June 2018

A man of letters

You can even read long words

Enjoy the book Will

G000269178

is
that
all
you
people
think
about
?

A Modern Haiku Collection

Gordon Gordon

◼ SQUARE PEG

1 3 5 7 9 10 8 6 4 2

Square Peg, an imprint of Vintage,
20 Vauxhall Bridge Road,
London SW1V 2SA

Square Peg is part of the Penguin Random House group
of companies whose addresses can be found at global.
penguinrandomhouse.com.

Penguin
Random House
UK

Illustrated by Vitoria Bastos & Matt Broughton

First published by Square Peg in 2017

www.vintage-books.co.uk

A CIP catalogue record for this book is available from the British
Library

ISBN 9781910931615

Printed and bound by Clays Ltd, St Ives plc

Penguin Random House is committed to a sustainable future
for our business, our readers and our planet. This book is made
from Forest Stewardship Council® certified paper.

FSC

CRAIG GOT HOME TO FIND
MATT SHITTING IN HIS BATHROOM,
WHICH IS HOW THEY MET.

Trevor's pregnancy
turned out to be wind. All the
journalists went home.

'I Collect sickbags!'

We were about to take off.
I put on headphones.

'Jacket still on fire.
Plz hurry up.' Chris texted
the fire department.

'I'm supposed to be at school. Yet here I am stuck burying this cow.'

Christine had no eyes.

She still drove though, such was her
hatred for cyclists.

Marge left flour and yeast
at the pond so Duck could make
his own fucking bread.

'I'm pregnant!' yelled June.

The crowds parted and June walked straight into the club.

His degree faked, his
tools homemade, one hand, and yet:
Surgeon of the Year.

The chickens rebelled,
shaved the farmer, and stuck a
lemon up his bum.

'Shit! The Sugababes!'

The women turned round. They were not the Sugababes.

Huw Edwards wrapped up
the news with a wink, then blew
a kiss, which spoiled it.

Henry the Hoover
smiled and cleaned. Later, someone
stuck their dick in him.

'It's a simple choice.
Either me and ALL my ants,
or – well, there's the door.'

JEFF TRAPPED HIS penis six times that DAY, MAKING HIM regret his THIRD WISH.

||||/ |

Mike sat at his desk,
remembered he was retired,
so took the day off.

**There was Jane, lording
it over those who couldn't
afford their own bees.**

'I swear to God mate.

Blow that bassoon one more time.

I fucking dare you.'

Bieber wrote a song.
The chorus was his PIN code
He lost everything.

Palpable Fury:
The Life of Delia Smith.
Out now in Hardback.

Sally Pipe (Dan's mum)
played spoons (uncredited) on
nine Bowie albums.

'I'm fucking famished!'
Exclaimed the caterpillar
in an early draft.

Dirk was no cowboy.
No hat, no horse, and the dust
set off his asthma.

'They have ALDI here!'
Chris parked the tank and, dodging gunfire, nipped inside.

'More! Oh God there's more!'
shrieked Liz, as another wave
of shitzus approached.

'And after the break,
it's Mary, Joseph, God and
a DNA test...'

JENNY PUT HER HEAD
RIGHT THROUGH, WHICH IF ANYTHING
MADE MATTERS MUCH WORSE

'Majestic creatures...'
Chris Packham groaned, before the swans finished him off.

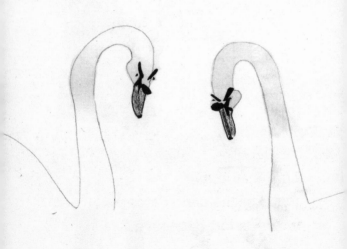

Lord Alan Sugar
made all the candidates wait
while his fart dispersed.

'We'll look back at this and laugh!' Promised the judge as he sentenced his wife.

Eddie Redmayne had prepped for the role of Godot for most of April.

'Surprise,' yelled Joseph
but the garden was empty
and it would soon rain.

At the office do
Troy dressed as Brett so he could
get off with Susan.

Getting into sheep
turned out to be hard in Bow
where it's all cafes.

'I know we're being
chased by a helicopter
Phillip. I'm not deaf.'

Sonic the Hedgehog
sobered up in the cell while
his agent was called.

Fran loved her dog, but
he only understood Welsh.
They walked in silence.

'NEVER SPEAK OF THIS'

Karen Brady told what was
left of the girls team.

'It's O Negative,'
said Dan, passing the thermos.
'So knock yourself out.'

In desperation,
Jack drank a whole bottle of
Mint Source shower gel.

'Like in *Moby-Dick*'
explained Mark, hoping that the
jury read widely.

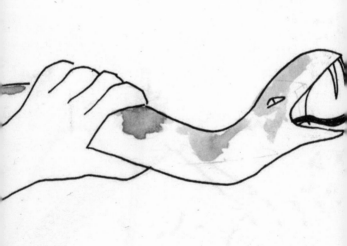

'UM YOU HAVE A SNAKE
ON YOUR...' JOHN STARTED, BUT THE
STEWARDESS WAS GONE

'Good Horse, Nice Horse. Stay.'
said Ruth, backing nervously
out of the bathroom.

RUMBLED, TRUMP TORE OFF
HIS HUMAN SUIT AND SCUTTLED
OUT OF THE BOARDROOM.

Susan lit her flare,
stood up in the pedalo
and hailed the tanker.

'Flippendo' slurred Dan.
The stool didn't move. Now he
owed them all a pint.

Hugh stuffed as many
as he could into the loft,
then hid the ladder.

Due to an error
the vegan meal was served on
a plate made of ham.

Thin Jim was *too* thin.
A gust picked him up and flew
him over Ealing.

Mary Poppins had
neither CRB checks, nor
the right work visa.

5ive reformed, but just
2 showed up, so they called it
2wo and no one came.

Ken checked his grenades.
Kiwis? Where were the grenades?
He phoned his son's school.

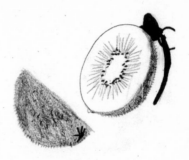

During the divorce
Mel brought up the doner wheel
Tim kept in the lounge.

The shrink ray had worked.
Now inside his plughole, Dan
weighed up the options.

'Look at my penis.'
But it was dark so no one
ever did see it.

To save costs, Corbyn
ran the Labour Party from
a bus stop in Penge.

Mike dropped his trousers.
Meg blushed and sat bolt upright.
Balls, thought Mike, too soon.

'Don't waste eggs,' said Cath.
But Jack just loved cracking them.
'It's the sound,' he said.

**Turkeys celebrate
their own version of Christmas
where they eat a man.**

Bob Marley was dug
up and made to play a gig.
'Three stars,' said *The Times*.

Tim was bad at texts.
His thumb was too big and he
never wrote nice things.

'Brilliant!' said John.
It was clear John had no clue
what kidney stones were.

John's wife of five years
turned out to be Noel Edmonds
playing a long prank.

Two trains and a swim.
The office commute was hell
from Clifford's new house.

MUD＊ PISS＊ BLOOD＊ SEMEN＊
This was no ordinary
Manchester derby.

Sue cancelled the rave.
She had catered for thirty
but thirty-nine came.

The Vicar sighed. Two
baptismal drownings this week.
There goes the licence.

'Lager?' asked Grandad.
'I'm eight,' answered Sam. 'Wine then?!'
Grandad was sweating.

The bath overflowed.
Bob suggested Anne get out.
Simon got out too.

'This bulb won't go till twenty twenty two!' Father chirped, screwing away.

'BUMHOLES!' YELLED THE QUEEN. THE PARTY STOPPED. THE QUEEN WAS STARTING TO SHOW OFF.

'Let's look at his knob!'
squeaked the surgeon. 'I'm awake,'
whispered Prince Philip.

'GUITAR!' CRIED THE EDGE
slapping his head and running
back into the Tube.

The Honey Monster
drove straight to Linda's, breaking
his bail conditions.

'I never got the
hang of that.' sighed Jim, watching
Roy pee standing up.

Darren kissed Julie
she was still behind the till
but he couldn't wait.

Jackson Pollock first painted as a joke. But then he was stuck with it.

Gregg Wallace ate the starter, then the plate, then the fork, then John Torode

I thought hard. Tone down
or enlarge the French accent?
She was still staring.

Years later, Arctic
explorers found Benedict
Cumberbatch alive.

'Sun, fun, sun and fun!'
The weatherman stood smiling.
He wrote his own scripts.

'All this damn football'
said Wenger during half-time
hoping they'd relax.

'No thanks, I've brought my own,' said Bear Grylls, taking out a flask of urine.

'I'm in here!' yelled Mum.
Hide and seek was spoilt again.
We never found Dad.

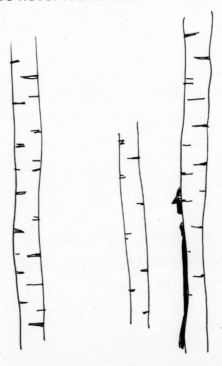

'And here are your gloves!'
Dave's one-year-old stood in goal.
Dave took a run up.

'Did you bring the flag?'
asked Neil. 'No, you said you had
packed it,' Buzz glared back.

Clive slept right through the
orgy. When he woke they'd gone.
Good nap though. Good nap.

No animal knows
who this 'Attenborough' is
or that he loves them.

Neil Armstrong farted.
Buzz Aldrin laughed. 'We'll go home,'
warned Michael Collins.

'MAKE ME GIANT SCONES. BIG ENOUGH TO SIT DOWN ON,'

Mary Berry snarled.

Beth broke up with Ben
on the Tube. Some passengers
tweeted pics of Ben.

Keats, Shelley and Blake
went to Butlins to write verse.
They mainly did odes.

'That's not how you bake!'
Ruth made her Dad put down the
chainsaw and the cat.

'Too fat to clean the windows of the Shard am I?!' The scaffolding creaked.

Sandra gave up wheat
Sadly she only ate wheat
and so quickly died.

Sting got bleach and tea confused. Six dead, including Pierce Brosnan and Cher.

Bruce and Hugh drew swords.
Passengers around them tensed.
Some got off at Bank.

'And the winner is...'
Daniel Day-Lewis muttered
as he opened bills.

'I'm *hugely* wealthy,'
the Queen flirted, knocking back
a second Pernod.

'Not again,' spluttered
Bill Oddie, brushing feathers
from his bloodied beard.

The Round Table cracked.
Arthur and the young knight froze
then dressed in silence.

'My name's Jemimah,'
lied Phil. His confidence grew,
'Jemimah Ball-Bag.'

'I'm posting myself!'
Scott yelled from inside the chest.
'Yes dear,' intoned Deb.

DIVORCED, beheaded, died. Divorced, beheaded, minced in escalator.

Suddenly Trevor
was leaving the club with the
puppies in his arms.

Geoff chose a 'porn cave'
as his one luxury on
Desert Island Discs.

'T?' a man called out.
The hangman shook his head and
climbed up the scaffold.

Alone with his thoughts,
Prince Charles reflected on the
scale of the killings.